"... that defines the light."

Anthony F. Pepe   D. Tori Morgenstein

PublishAmerica
Baltimore

First printing

Cover art: *Stella*, oil on canvas, 30x32, c2005 by Lauren Pasarella.

ISBN: 1-4137-4218-1
PUBLISHED BY PUBLISHAMERICA, LLLP
www.publishamerica.com
Baltimore

Printed in the United States of America

This book is dedicated to:
those that need it,
those that deserve it
and those that have it coming!

Acknowledgments

We would like to thank; Kate, NSU and Azim.

Tori would like to thank: my beloved sister, my most cherished, C.C. (Cherisse Morgenstein) my mother, my aunt, Jennifer, Danny Boy and Charlie. Sensei Mike Mitchele, Lauren (my kitten) Pascarella, Anthony Pepe for his much-needed and drawn on friendship and support. And to Sara Elizabeth Zeko, the love even she can't kill.

And with special thanks to Dr. Marianne Lawless, for ending my life and showing me a new one.

Anthony would like to thank: Jeanette for showing me the poet inside, Mom, Dad, Julie, Uncle Mike, Patti and Alana. Thank you, Grandma. Tori Morgenstein for completing the circle and helping to break the cycle. Lauren gets another shout here 'cause she's Lauren. Thank you to the countless others that have been there from the get go and the newfound support of Stef

Table of Contents

Catalyst - 9
A toast - 10
No More - 11
Warrior-ism - 12
So They Say - 13
Cognition - 16
Old Eyes - 17
Untitled - 18
Exit Womb - 19
Do I ? - 20
Color-blind - 21
Reporting Live - 22
While you were sleeping - 23
2 Young 2 be 4 - 24
I See - 25
ReCognition - 26
Rise Up - 27
Right To The Point - 29
Pains List - 30
Terrorlies - 32
My Sword - 33
What Did You Do - 35
Your Will - 36
By Choice - 38
The Gauntlet - 39
The Wall - 40
Cycles - 41
Jennifer - 43
Mommy's Little Daddy - 44
Simple Question - 46
Childish Grievances - 47
Poetry Beast - 49
Lesser Than Evil - 51

Dark Silence - 52
Simple Truth - 54
Time To Simmer - 55
Gambling Hearts - 56
Words Lost - 57
Sunday Mornings - 59
Date Rape - 61
De-constructing Self - 62
Poetry Slam - 63
Judgement - 64
Potential Patricide - 66
Dying Light - 67
Sunlight - 69
This Is My Life - 70
Bound - 71
Remember Me This - 72
Still Here - 73
Surrender - 74

Catalyst

For some reason, there's no need
to mention bad intentions, when I show
my face someplace
If someone has any sort of guilty conscience
it tends to show on their face, in my presence
Comfort levels itch, twitch, and burn
with a single discerning gaze, cast to disparage
any guilty party
There is this part of me, that can smell
the root of a disparity in energy
and seeks to level the playing field more toward equality

I am a walking litmus test, except
at my best, I don't need to touch you
to expose you
I am the catalyst that causes
the involuntary disclosure
of inner demon exposure
Exorcizing lies from behind disguises stripped
Monsters seem to ponder their fate
when the direction of my intention is announced
The offense of their oppression is trounced
into submission, and the ensuing regression
leads them to the defensive postures
that ensure me, that my postulations were just
But I digress,
For there is no need for me to
cast farther accusatory commentary
toward those transgressors
who now wear their unmentionables
on their face

Anthony F. Pepe

A toast

To a great and awesome God
To truly being God's creation
To being Godlike, yet Godforsaken
To being fundamentally evil, To being spiritually corrupt
To racial diversity never seeing indifference,
To kindly being asked to shut the fuck up
To the lines that we make, To ignorance being able to talk
To live as if dead, To be dead and still walk
To the ego, the superego, but mostly to the id
To the girl crying in the shower,
trying to wash off what her father did
To the inconvenience of actually
having to take time to raise a child
To the mothers who turned the other cheek
while their daughters were defiled
To a child molester's sanctuary, the Roman Catholic Church
To all you dumb fucks who thought it couldn't get any worse
To all those who agree: that little slut got what she deserved
To the nightly need to be so drunk that he slurs every word
To harmonious intercourse, to STDs
To the judge who proclaimed it was her fault,
calling her promiscuous and a tease.
To the cup being half empty, unless it's half full
To Sadistic Socialism, Capitalistic Treachery,
To the bliss of being a fool
To only being able to see a woman's body in a sexual manner
To endangered animal hides hanging from coat hangers
To none of this shit making any sense
To the activists and insurgents who gave up,
and now just walk a fence

D. Tori Mrogenstein

like so many others she's been shamed
assigned ownership and blame
abashed, the rain covers her like a stain
and an open casket cannot explain
why she'll never again walk through your door
everywhere parents treating their child like a whore
saying it's what she was asking for ...
penetrating and desecrating her until she's sore ...
until in an action she ended it all, all the note said was,
                    "no more ..."

D. Tori Morgenstein

Warrior-ism

Sometimes, the harder
you fight
the more you wonder what
it would be like
to surrender

Anthony F. Pepe

So they say

A man has to be strong
.........ALWAYS
On the battlefield belongs
.........To SLAY
Surrender up to something
...NEVER
His purpose is conquering
...FOREVER
So they say
So I've been told
So I've heard
His valor proven every
DAY
Must be dominant in his
HOLD
Never to speak a submissive
WORD
Not supposed to understand
flowers and butterflies
bridal showers and how to cry
So I've been told
Not for him to want
to answer to
another
Quiet cuddling and romantic nuzzling
Not for him to understand
So I've heard
Not allowed to want to
....SERVE
Standing up with all his
...NERVE
Never giving up
...CONTROL
Always maintaining his dominant

13

ROLE
never let them see him
cry
Not supposed to be sweet
why?
So they say
All a fallacy
SO SAYS ME!!!!!!!!
I am man's man
Crush you with bare hands
then cry over your remains
Let you know I'm the BOSS
then thank you for
surrendering
I get MY point across
even if it means
whispering
When I hurt
…Tell ME
not to CRY
for surely you
………..MAY DIE!!!!
When I put on an apron
for someone to serve
and show the sweetness within
…Go Ahead
……Step Up!
…….SHOW ME YOUR NERVE!!!!!!
tell ME I'm not supposed to
kneel
For my Wrath you will then
feel
……SO SAYS ME!!!!!!!!
……….SO SAYS I!!!!!!!
It's easy to Crush those things
softer
Mistake Kind for Weak
…showing Love left to the

....Meek

To surrender to something
Weak
Is something for Strong men
to seek
............SO SAYS ME!!!!!!!!!!
SO SAYS I!!!!!!!!!

Anthony F. Pepe

Cognition

sometimes, if you're lucky, and if you're ready ... something will break
      something inside you will break free
and you'll wonder: what is the reason?
           and find one
but is it the right reason?   Is it?
      Is it a part; is it a part of a part... is it?
Maybe the wind broke it, and freed you
maybe it was the wind that forced it to break
      the wind has a way of applying pressure ... ineffable deafening
pressure,
      blowing dry the moisture from within, drying til hollow
maybe it broke off you because it was never really a part of you in the first
place.
      Maybe it was done with you,
         your benevolence
            your ambivalence,
               Or maybe you were done with it,
                 Maybe it was your *Cognizance*
Your paperback landscape was no test, no lesson, No maker of men.
      Which is why the lie you've been living, will never be lived again ...

D. Tori Morgenstein

16

Old Eyes

These old eyes
 cry
These old eyes
 cry for all the lives
 they've seen lost
 not to earth
 but to time
These old eyes
 cry for times
  amounting to
  seven lives
   worth of lives
   lost to time

Anthony F. Pepe

Untitled

steady dripping silence, amply filling up the cup, amble out pour of violence, while we desperately sway, "enough is enough." possibility is to choice, what love is to divorce … please tell which is worse: to see a seed removed from the sacred soil to which it's bound, or watch as a tree is cut and falls to the ground …

and if it does fall, and no one is there to hear it, will it still make a sound?

D. Tori Morgenstein

Exit womb

Her skin was candy-coated, her flavor was opiate … I was dealing, but I was not coping with it … at times she was a sedative, but she usually just kept me strung out … her voice reminded me of a cello, quiet yet resonant, and slow as it traveled, following me from one room to the next, as if she saw me in a checkmate that I did not detect … and so I moved, I stirred, it's as she once said to myself: I've never met a soul, who ever got what they deserved … her lips were just icing, her tongue was just cake, she placed me in her oven, she wanted me to bake …

Because it's all been done for nothing, but it wasn't quite free,

You see I am an open book, but pages are missing …

Her lips stick to everything, company while I was working, but her lips would tremble and her stick would smear, when her nightmares would wake her and turn reality to fear … mascara tear tracks, stripping gears into more thumbtacks for her to crucify herself with … she was a scratching post for her memories, she was a wet-nap for the centuries … jail times the second handed crimes, on a broken mirror she cut more lines … she was my crestfallen tapestry, who would lie to me through the teeth of her piety … she would drive me to the point of breaking, only to save me for baking … peal her body off the tile, take her to bed, I tried to talk but her voice was a cello, so I just closed my eyes and listened to what she said … because sometimes her lips were just her icing, her tongue as moist as cake, and the longer I stayed in her oven, the more I began to bake …

So we've all been done for nothing, but nothing is for free,

Take a look, I am an open book, I'll leave your eyes burning …

And the fire's shadow was dancing on the ground, children were covering their ears to muffle the sirens' sounds, the flames paraded along the walls, and they were waltzing to the sound of he crowd's catcalls, the red paint melted off the blue it was painted over in the strip club's bathroom stalls … and the smokes shadow slid horizontal like the shadow of a ghost, reaching the reflection off a puddle that was just shallow enough for her to make it across …

D. Tori Morgenstein

Do I?

Do I, want to
feel needed
or
Need to
feel wanted
and
If I have to
desire either
Do I truly
have either

Anthony F. Pepe

Color-blind

In this world it's all a matter of point of view
And through my eyes, no one else can see you
The way that I used to
The way I saw the world in you
The future in you
My heart in you
Not to mention the way I now see you
For it is all a matter of point of view
Like showing the color-blind the sky is blue
Or lung cancer showing the smoker what it will do
A recovered addict showing the junky what the needle will do
Is like trying to explain Quantum Physics to
Little Boy Blue
A paranoid schizophrenic doesn't see the friend in you
For it's all a matter of point of view
And sometimes we have to change our point of view
To just get through, and that I do
Still I long for the day you see the sky as blue
So I can once again see you
The way I used to

Anthony F. Pepe

Reporting Live

I want to set the record straight
about the words I write
They do not come from special insight
I merely recite
The things around that I have seen
and of things felt by me
That is all I offer thee
A report, an account, a record this be
Is as it does seem to me
All I have to offer thee
If any special credit be mine
of my words of Fancy Flight
I look at all the gray we see
and put it down in Black and White.

Anthony F. Pepe

While you were sleeping

a large hand on a small thigh
squeezing tighter, her tearing eye
unable to stop, deeper he pried …
All within the privacy of your own lie …

D. Tori Morgenstein

I lived with a Halloween mask.

My mother worked late a lot. She had a man living with her. I lived with her, too. The man did not have a job, so he was in the house a lot. I was in the house a lot, too …

I think I was three, I was too young to be four …

The man who lived with my mother had two faces.

He was very mean to me, the man, and my mother worked very late. The Halloween mask was mean to me too. It use to chase me. I remember running from the it. The mask would chase me screaming and breathing, and I would fall. Always I'd fall.

The man who lived with us would take things from me. The man would rip my toys from my hands and put them places. My favorite toys. He would put them out of my reach. I remember reaching out for them. The man was always taking things from me.

I must have been three, I was too young to be four.

I had a toy Spider Man doll; he was my favorite. I called him Spidy. I always slept with Spidy would protect me while I was sleeping …

Not always,

The Halloween mask use to take Spidy from me. The Halloween mask liked to take things from me, just like that man. I remember running. The mask was like an animal. I could hear it breathing. I never got away. I remember something burning me. The Halloween mask with the teeth was yelling at me; *screaming!* I could smell its breath. I could smell the growling and screaming. I couldn't find the Spidy. I remember reaching out for Spidy. Something was burning me. It had teeth. It was yelling; *screaming!* I could smell it's breath. I could smell the burning.

I remember all the things the man would take from me.

My toys … Spidy.

My mother worked late a lot.

I think I was three; I was too young to be four.

D. Tori Morgenstein

I See

I can see the words in your eyes
before you speak them
I can hear the words in your breath
before you think them
I can see the monkeys on your back
before you feel them
I can feel the load you carry
by the way you walk
I can hear the words that hurt you
in the way you talk
I can see the shame you feel
on the clothes you wear
I can see your fears
weigh your shoulders down
I think volumes
about your frowns
I see things, in little things about you,
that you didn't know were your things
I hear things and feel things surround you
that made you put that wall around you
It's time you put those things behind you
and let me remind you
That the Sun shines bright
and there is Love all around you.

Anthony F. Pepe

ReCognition

How many times must I
bleed for you
before you see, that I would
die for you
How many times must I
bleed for you
before I see, that I am
dying for you

Anthony F. Pepe

Rise Up

I want to start a revolution
Rise up and start a movement
But I'm not tryin' to save no tree
or chanting about racial issues that
chain us to shackles past.
"Animal rights! Animal rights!"
Ain't the fight for me
Can you, tell me, why we,
feel we, need to,
landscape the garden
And ignore the home
   and the problems within
    ?
Stop them from burning the Rainforest
while the bedroom's ablaze!
Crimes against innocence
Those practiced at turning blind eyes
Attitudes that let this exist
is the heart of why all our problems persist

You want to, try to stop a war
While hands are raised in the name of love

Beating women like slaves
treating children like pets
From Beverly Hills to Watts,
Fifth Ave. To Avenue B
and you want to tell me
"Meat is Murder!"
"Hug a Tree"

You see there are over
100 Million women in this country
and all most 18% have been victims of

sexual assault
and over 22% have been victims
of some form of physical abuse
That makes up 40% of the female population
and guess what
64% of the perpetrators
that committed these heinous acts
Were either
Current partners

Former partners

Or Family members

Now you do the math
and while you do, keep in mind that
This statistical cross section
    Of our Nation represents
    Reported cases
And it is estimated that about
1 in 3 cases ever get reported

Now tell me what cause
needs more attention than this
Because I'm telling you
You can't even dream
of fixing anything else

While hands are raised
in the name of Love!

Anthony F. Pepe

Right to the Point

Let's get right to the point
The medieval forms of, evil performed on, innocent lives
Over the years, have built up such fears, and rained down in tears
That burn at my soul
And I want you to know
That the medieval forms of evil to be performed on your soul
For those innocents lost to your depravity, could never be enough
To touch the surface of the reparations,
due those touched by you aberrations
So begin your preparations
For the perpetual cycle of hate you have perpetrated throughout the ages
Ends with you, stops today
If dare I say, I am coming for you, searchin' you out with words
I'm chasing you down, running through crowds
These words hanging over you like clouds
Everywhere you turn you will learn
You will be faced with the faces you have defaced, 'cause now
I'm in your face
Every corner you turn, there I speak, into your thoughts I seep
Gonna leave you weepin', you will get no reprieve, you will receive
The endless unwavering verbal assault I send after you
Then I'm gonna salt those wounds, make you expose you
You will have no choice but to show your true colors
You will show others, what you are, with your eyes, when you hear my
voice
In your car on the morning drive, in the bar hanging with the guys
When you change the station 'cause you don't like it
When you leave the bar 'cause you can't take it
Whatcha gonna do, when people see you for you
And you can't fake it

Anthony F. Pepe

29

Pains List

Let me see
What would I do to thee
if given opportunity
how would I make you pay
let me count the ways
    ONE
For every fingerprint
You left where it didn't
belong
    TWO
for those things that you forced
lesser to do to you
3 - Third eyes penetrated
    FOUR
the innocent lives
that you desecrated
5 - minds intimidated
6 - Passing on your hatred
    SEVEN
Shadows that you hide in
Let me see
What would I do to thee
If given opportunity
How would I make you pay
Let me count the ways
For every fingerprint
Forced and penetrated
Innocent lives that mind
Hatred
Infinite shadows you
Cast
You tell me how

You should
Pay for
Your past

Anthony F. Pepe

Terrorlies

Time to apologize to those you terrorize
Running around living those lies, covering eyes
Despising and demonizing those that let their hands rise
You think you're not a monster 'cause you don't beat her
But you make weapons of the words you say to her
Demoralizing words or physical blows, we know both
Leave wounds and woes
What do think happens when you tell a child that they are
"Worthless, stupid, never gonna amount to nothing"
Do you think they grow up feeling like they are amazing
"I wish I never had you, you ruined my life"
What do you think those words do to the rest of their life
For every word you've said in hate I condemn you
May every pain you caused with words be brought
down on you three times three
May the pain of your every word haunt your every dream
"You bitch, you slut, you whore"
May the pain of such words rain down on you
And leave you writhing on the floor

Anthony F. Pepe

My Sword

My pen hits the paper with the resounding echo
of the millions of screams and cries
not heard over thousands of years!

The force with which I apply pigment to pulp,
far greater than the forces that have beat
past truths to a pulp!

I wield the feather of my quill like the power of a tornado
that pushes straw through stop signs, as its lines
cut through the steel armor of ignorance
and the walls of deceit and oppression!

Its shaft not wavering under the load of stone lids,
I pry off of third eyes!

I balance upon its tip the very berth of the world
and all its hopes and dreams!

I use it to lay open the belies of lies,
so wide, with such ease that blind eyes can see!

I shoot words from it that strike like lighting with their electricity,
the intensity of which rolls on like thunder through the ages!

I swing it like a club to break open the shells,
of small men that hide behind big things!

But it is not about me, or my pen
for as it is just an instrument of words
I am but the mechanism that operates the instrument!

I unsheathe it, to unleash the word upon the vast blank expanse of the
sheet
only, for the word has no other way to appear there
and the pen has no other way to leave it there!

Anthony F. Pepe

What Did You Do

I know what you do, I see you , smell you,
See it in your eyes, behind closed doors, through closed eyes
What Did You Do
Get your hands off of her, put your hands up
And step away from the child you sick son of a bitch
This ain't gonna be mild, if I got my hands on you
For death you would wish and wish and wish
Look at me when I'm talking to you
Yeah you, and you and you and you

There it goes it's happening again, some sick son of a bitch
Just smacked his wife
That's alright enjoy it while you can, 'cause if I got my hands on you
……… begging for your life
What's the matter, people, can't you see it, can't you hear it
Can't you feel it?
You don't see her crying, hear children screaming,
Feel innocence dying?
Keep running your mouths saying everything's OK
'cause I know you're lying
And I'm just trying to shed some light
Shed some light on the quiet people's plight
I know that they say silence is golden
But silence is what keeps on holding them
Hold on a minute, before we get into it, before I rip into you
This is your last chance 'cause I know someone else put this
Sickness into you, and not just the sickness that makes you do it
But the sickness that makes them, do nothing about it
I don't want to destroy you, but I will
If that is the only way I can stop you

Anthony F. Pepe

35

Your Will

You can't turn away from me now, I wont let you turn your face
It is I, your child grown, it is I your disgrace
make believe I was man enough to live in your shadow
pretend I was strong enough to be your coward
proud enough to do everything you say
and independent enough to do it all your way
to me, if any, what words would you have to say

I was still a baby when away you gave me
changed my name, then you blamed me
you sadistic fuck, it's like you framed me
all my life you overlooked all my strengths
you never noticed the roads I traveled and their great lengths
it was everything I could do growing up to get your affection
it was everything I could do to breathe the night you almost caved my chest
in

living with you I feared for my life
you and your fucking wife …
your fist to my face
you said I was the disgrace
you chose her over me
with every word she said the harder you hit me
then you said I was a pussy because I was bleeding
I remember looking up at you gasping and heaving
you looked me in the eye
you said, "You're no son of mine"
for years I told no one, this secret was mine
I hid the bruises from my mother to protect you every time
now you actually have the balls to try to tell me I'm no longer your son
motherfucker I wish that were true, and I'm not the only one
so listen up, old man, because I've had my fill

and I've no desire to be in your will
my only regret when you die
will be that it wasn't me who got credit for the kill

D. Tori Morgenstein

By Choice

I fought back, my father in life
immortal by choice, I had the right
to believe in this, to stay all night
something he gave, took away my sight

black n blue, he blackened me too
forgotten things and places I've been
too many faces, too many dreams
was it too much or was I unwise
who did it worse? who can say why?
now pushing back all these tears and fighting back all the time,
I try and lose myself in this simple rhyme.

I fought back, my father in life
immortal by choice, I had the right
hungry like a vampire, running from the light
corruption runs too deep, to ever make this right

"he comes from a room that shakes"
"he echoes from a heart that breaks"
"this life would not embrace"
"see the things he tries to take."
"so I run from every trace, "
"every trace of this place"
"so now I run,"

D. Tori Morgenstein

The Gauntlet

Oh no, here I go again using my words to separate foe from friend
You're either with me or against me
If you're not part of the solution you're part of the pollution
Polluting minds, passing time, walking around on very thin little white lines
I'm here to separate the men from the bitches
And when I get through with you you'll be wishin'
For witches, to take this curse off you
Remove this hex from you
'cause I'm opening eyes to let people see you for you
With that I curse you
And there ain't no witch that can take this curse off of you
Just be happy you're not looking for
some one to take my hands off you
But I won't do that see, I'm not gonna let any part of you
Seep into me
I'm on a mission now, gonna leave you wishin' I
never picked up a pen, or turned on a light
Don't step up 'cause I don't want to fight
But if you make me defend myself, I will do it right
I want to do this piece in the middle of a prison yard
Naked, without the guards
I want to look out at the crowd and see all the
Pedophiles, rapists and wife-beating bitches looking down at the ground
What's the matter, big guy, can't look me in the eye
Feeling dirty, feeling guilty, you wanna cry, go run and hide
Can't hide from my words, I'm calling your name are you feeling the shame
What's that, I can't hear you, you don't like it when someone
doesn't fear you, you got something to say
You think you're tough, if you really want to do it that way
I'm calling your bluff
But I'd rather brand you, let everyone see you
Let you feel the shame and victims' pains
And give you one last chance to change your evil ways

Anthony F. Pepe

39

The Wall

You're
Ruthlessly feeding on
those defensively cowering from
the manifestations of
your insecurities and
inadequacies
Preying on the innocent and weak
to make yourself feel
Bigger and Badder
Sometimes I wish I wasn't
so enlightened
and I could show you
How it feels to be frightened
    Sometimes I just want to
    Kick Some Ass
But, don't think this
offensive, this is defensive
But I will henceforth
Defend innocence to the
Death
So the next time you
think about hitting
someone who's 3
or generally weaker than thee
Think about this
One of these days
To get to them
You may have to
Go through me

Anthony F. Pepe

Cycles

I beseech you, I don't hate you, I just want to reach you
But I would crush you if I had to
I want to teach you, not learn you a lesson
I want to teach you lessons I learned the hard way
I walk around every day watching people banging their heads
banging their heads against the same wall
and it's like I'm the only one that can see it all
They can't see, you can't see, they can't see you, you can't see them
but I see you, I see you all, just banging your heads
And when I try to give you a pillow, you want to see me fall

You see, I've been though it all, been there done that
banged all the walls, took all the falls
Been tied down, held back, beat up, shot up, drunk
Been tore up, chewed up, spit out, punked
I know what it feels like to be you, all of you
I've felt all your pains, played all your games
Been left out cold in the rain, didn't eat for days
looked through the haze and learned the hard way
I had to change my ways
Just banging your heads and ridding the merry-go-round,
but it ain't merry round here you just go round and round and round
Rolling through cycles locked inside circles
acting like love will bite you, and
If you don't learn to want to break them even I can't help you
I beseech you, please let me reach you
Just break the cycle, you know what to do
'cause even a million dollars ain't worth what you do
Put down your works, I know it hurts
but if you don't do it now it just gets worse and worse and worse
Forget the clothes, forget the dough, forget your woes
'cause we've all had times in our lives that we felt like hoes
Who knows, I know, 'cause there are thousands of ways we let people pay
to see the different degrees, they can put us on our knees

41

So break that cycle, step back take a good hard look through you
Not at you, let you forgive you
Don't let past hate seal your future fate
Let you nurture you into something great

Anthony F. Pepe

Jennifer

she used to take stage for the gazing appreciation of raping eyes ... vile, vulgar vicarious versions of her father sliding dollar bills between her thighs ... she's reenacting a childhood, allowing people to do to her all the things her father would ... after work, ammonia and brillo pad of soft steel wool to scrub herself clean with as if she could ... she's pushing me away, self inflicting wounds, crucifying herself to a tree, cutting herself like wood ...

if I had the means, if knew which ones ... I'd make a bloodbath out of all of them ... because she's crying in her sleep again, the nightly nightmares have begun ... until waking then raking her bare skin till it's bloody, thinking she's dirty, desperately scratching with feverous fury that feeling from her body ... fingerprints like acid burns, I try to help but away she turns ...

after rape, came an abortion when her wife-beating ex-husband came back for a second portion ... as if she was his for the taking, now she's fearing his from prison escaping ... she's injesting absolution, fuel for the fire to feed the delusions ... five limes times some red red rum then stir the solution ... us on a houseboat offshore key west, with no life vest, only us in isolation ... that was never our expectation, just our nightly conversation, while using barstools to hold up our farfetched conditions, and her avoiding the topic of her baker act detentions ...

if only I could go back, and stop the treachery of his fatherly trysts ... if only I could fix all this shit with my fist ... if only I wasn't so helpless to save her from the razor's scars of incision, elbow to wrist ...

she left me with more than memories and no contact ... she poured the remains of a bottle of coke that was flat, into a half empty gallon of jack ... she then drank it like that, and that Sunday morning south beach, never gave her back ...

and it's called the "trauma connection," and all of it is fact ...

D. Tori Morgenstein

Mommy's Little Daddy

As I speak, there is a woman somewhere
 teaching her little boy
  to be just like her daddy
Daddy's little girl, showing Mommy's little boy
 that she is still, just a toy
  for men, like her father, their father
   reinforcing habits learned, unknown
    yet set in stone
              of flesh defiled
Little boys shown from the get go
"Daddy says, 'Mommy's a ho'"
Misconstrued, confused emotions of
Attention = Affection = Love
But when the only attention received
 in her formative years, was the back of a hand
  and the affection and love received
   was just a little, too deeply seeded
    something goes wrong with the long term
     definitions of such words
A misfiring of feelings from
 seemingly wrongful manifestations
  of emotions, so to speak
   so she seeks out all that
    she knows as normal
     an informal education in
      degradation for her
        offspring, her seed
You see, we all have our own
 sense of perceived normalcy
  and we all have a need, to proceed down a path
   follow a course marked out, ahead of us
    and it may not be our fault
     that our teachers have deceived us
      set us in the wrong direction

But how much recognition do you need
  to see that the road ahead
  is too dark and in need of repair
Did you really think that your
  special brand of despair was, your teacher' invention
  did you ever wonder how,
it,
 got,
   there
From whence it came, from hence you relay
  and still today, women are teaching their sons
  to be, just like, their fathers

Anthony F. Pepe

Simple Question

Is he
the man
you want
your son
to be

Anthony F. Pepe

46

Childish Grievances

it never took place, that never happened, no matter how many men your mother put you through, it just never happened, no, not to you, her only son, her number one, look, enough, it's done, it's through, this conversation is over, or at least that's what she would tell you ... she would tell that you were her little man, but you just couldn't understand, if your mommy had you then why did she need all these others, these adults who were in competition for your mother's attention, see, they hated you and that's exactly what they told her, these grown men who loved to intimidate you, and perpetuate the burden she left on your shoulder ... they shamed you while she worked late, took the food from off your plate, covered your mouth with duck tape, you were too much of a pussy to fight back, too stupid to call it rape, it was too late for you, you had no one to save or emancipate you from these demons who would dominate you, create wounds that would never heal as they would penetrate you, articulate new ways to desecrate you, lock you in dark rooms for hours to isolate you, stain you and shame you to forever seal your fate, so you push back the tears, fast forward the years, and feel it all churn to hate

she loved you but she failed you, she hugged you but she didn't protect you, you were just a child, incest was your plague, and your innocence was defiled, in these marriages of convenience, you were an inconvenience, with petty complaints, childish grievances, parent child role reversal, it was supposed to be real life, but it was treated more like a fuckin' rehearsal ... so as you grew you hated her, you never understood the impact this patriarchy had on her, that she was a target, that you were seen as garbage, instead you just grew colder, your father was a saboteur, the world was a maze of locked and unlocked doors, your mother was treated like a whore, while you were just the bastard son she was too stupid to abort, all this continued until you were old enough to walk out the door, and to this day, it still echoes, nightmares and dreams keep crashing at your shore, never still, never silent, never sober, because for you there is no cure ...

but shame is not your only option, those monsters are still out there, and you can stop them, you can write and flow, get in their face, and let them all know, you can speak out against, you can stand up for, and when he tries to lay his hand on her you can kick in the door, because they are not just victims, or statistics, and neither are you, so get up, stand up, motherfucker, you got work to do...

D. Tori Morgenstein

Poetry Beast

Sometimes, Poetry gets the better
of me
Grabs hold of me and
I open my mouth and
it's like there's an
Army of me
waiting to attack,
step you back
The Troops are assembled and
they're getting hungry for
verbal retribution
Intimidation retaliation
I can't
hold them back
They snap
your head back
with their roar
I open my mouth and
out this
barrage pours

I speak about Peace
yet unleash
a beast
All teeth and
claws the words
themselves
Stretching my jaws
cracking my skull
twisting my spine
Like
I'm outta my mind
They will get their point across
no matter the cost

to me
my psyche
My body
A submissive slave
to the wave
of emotion
behind the
Message
    That chose
    To flow
    Through me

Anthony F. Pepe

Lesser Than Evil

Here we go, it's tough love time
I want to know how we were schooled
to be fooled into this frame of mind
to enable us to rationalize even our own demise
How do we determine that the lesser of two evils
is any less detrimental to our mental state
You see, the human mind is great at self preservation
and it reserves the right to delude you into thinking
your lesser of, is still above
some other

Because believe you me,
the Junky takes great pride
in not being a pusher
And those Pets pose,
but don't get down
'cause they ain't no hoes
And even the Pedophile,
swells with self-righteousness
because he's no Cannibal
But we're all accountable
for our own,
lesser thans

Anthony F. Pepe

Dark Silence

There are things in this world
I refuse to unfurl
Subject matter that no matter
what I write
onto which I will shed no light
For to lend them the levity my pen
would leverage them
would attempt deniability
of the severity of such atrocities
I must not speak of pains injected
things inflicted me
in little more than infancy
I can not think of women subjected
minds infected
by sick demonic supposed intimacy
I will not think of
wraith that I would
see brought down on
those purveyors of such monstrosities
Never mind what they would feel from me
I must not, I will not, I cannot think of these things
I must not, I will not, I cannot speak of these things
I must not, I will not, I cannot feel the hate that this brings

I will not ,I cannot, I must not
I must not, I cannot, I will not
I will not, I will not
I will not lie to myself any more
For
you see atrocities such as these
happen to all kinds of people
even people like me
So maybe it's up to people like me
to see to it that this never happens again

to anybody
Now I'm not talking about a path
of retaliation or retribution
No, rather think of this as
an intervention
an intervention of reckoning
and I reckon this needs to start immediately
because I feel like I can only
fight this fight for so long
peacefully
for in the end it comes down to this

If you think some of the stuff I
scream about can make your flesh creep
You should hear some of the shit
I still whisper in my sleep

Anthony F. Pepe

Simply the truth.

The mistakes my mother made, were at least made because she loved me ...
Where as the mistakes my father made, were made only because he was angry ...

D. Tori Morgenstein

Time to simmer

He wiped his feet on a sheet made of splinters off my backbone, that was crushed by the way his paper works, then he mocked me, the feeble jerk, that jerked at his lines, ensnared in the reasons he had to concur to divide, but not all equations are divisible, just like not all religions are forgivable, relive-able walks through his pitiful pitfalls, his poisonous prosecution, silence is a waste product of violence, it's unheard pollution, I was just one of the many children buildin' a subconscious out of burnt matches and hand-me-downs, with hell as a hostage, aspersed and accosted, and constant reminders of all I was not, I was just the underline, lining, while he was constantly reminding me that I was not defining what he called a son ...

Turn the heat down, cover, allow time to simmer, allow skin to grow over splinters, go and visit him for the summer, then again in the winter, go with him to visit your brother in prison, but no one was there, I wanted so bad to be a part, but I was unrelated, I was belated to my own blood, he was my father but I was not his son, well, I was until I turned 21 and he told me what a disgrace I had become ...

D. Tori Morgenstein

Gambling Hearts

I've written hundreds of lines
 filled with rhymes, about the times
  and ways you brought me pains
   no words can explain
The things that I went through
 to continue to breath
Countless hours devoured by
 dealing with the hand I was dealt
The pain that I felt
 the times that I knelt
  in the dirt, and begged the
   dust to make it stop
    then reveling in the strength
    that I got, for it didn't kill me
    and that strength filled me
For every pound of pain
 I got an ounce of strength
  275 lbs. of ounces of strength
  so strong for so long
   that I longed for
    some pain, just to see
    if I could feel it

Who would have thought that
 after all the cards you dealt
  the worst pain I could have felt
   was not over hands I was dealt
    but rather,
     knowing you were playing the same hand
     in the same losing game.
Don't you know that no matter how
 the cards are shuffled
  and who cuts the deck
   the house always wins.

Anthony F. Pepe

Words Lost

The lost words of poets lost
to tangled pasts
Mangled memories of brilliant metaphors
locked behind steel doors of
diseased minds
Lines too twisted by troubled times
to find their way to paper
Thoughts that raced so fast
to be erased before spoken
Distant memories of the reasons they never wrote them
Inspirations reverberations so sped to be stilled
The muse so consuming to cause one
to lose all reasoning
Pains that brought madness instead of greatness
Solitary silence in the sounds of too many screams
heard too loud to understand a single word
speech beaten beyond the reaches of spoken word
Expression repressed from fear of
possible retaliation from the one that pressed
every word there

You see
I know this, my best words
come from my worst pains
My darkest places shine the brightest lights
It's my deepest emotions
that illicit the greatest motion in those hearts
that choose to sit within
the reach of my expression
I know the things that I've withstood
to bring the understanding I have today
I know the places in my past
that I have stood on the edges of my sanity
And the path I followed to find my way back

to find myself wondering
About the lost words
of poets lost to tangled pasts

Anthony F. Pepe

Sunday Mornings

It's just what happed to you … it's not who you are.

She never understood my love for Sunday mornings.
She didn't understand the magic of mourning.
She was so much more than a beautiful shell, she was mystical and sensual, but she just didn't get Sunday mornings …

She was a glasshouse in a hailstorm, she was an American beauty, stillborn … her tears seeped through the leers of her spiraling formative years.
She says it's easier to understand her, if one thinks of her as a liar.
She thinks the days will pass by smoother,
if she can just act a little bit number …
She says she won't be inconvenienced, and she can't be loved,
because beautiful and sensual are just other types of drugs …
She says that hunger doesn't really hurt,
and that to a bulimic everything is dessert.
She only swallows more than she can take, and she only snorts what she's unwilling to waste.
She says that the everything she sees and survives,
only adds another question mark to why she's alive.
And she wouldn't let me finish, when I tried to tell her no one could take her innocence, I never got to explain to her that it was a crime against her, that the ones who were guilty were the perpetrators, the ones who offered her a drink around a quarter past four … and when she came to, a quarter till two, hemorrhaging privately, randomly discarded in a Rascal House diner's bathroom stall …
She said the one who found her called for help …

and the help that found her,
did nothing at all ...

And I love her ...

D. Tori Morgenstein

Date Rape

I've tried to find a clever, witty way to address this
subject, but I find myself at a loss for words.
So I'll keep it simple.
Date rape, in my dictionary is not defined as:
" A woman lacking the correct cautionary vocabulary as
to prevent her interest from being misconstrued as lewd."
Where the fuck does it say that a kiss is an invitation
for penetration?
Tell me!!!
Where does it say, that if you don't put up a "fight"
you give up your right to, say "no."
Let's see, how does it go?
You're faced with a situation where you were naive enough
to actually "trust" somebody. Shame on you!
You weren't cynical or jaded enough to realize that
he was one of those guys.
You were unable to see below the surface to see
the predatory creature lurking there.
So, you take your lack of foresight and or judgement thereof
and somehow twist it around to meaning he was right
and the blame lies with you,
the shame hides in you.
Well, I've got news for you.
In my eyes it's clear where the blame lies and
I despise the fact that, not only did this happen to you
but, he found some way to make you blame you.
And I have to wonder, how many of you, he has under his belt?
And how many more he needs to score before one of you
    Speak up, and put a stop to them!!!!

Anthony F.Pepe

Deconstructing Self

My sister, my friend, she took it to her head, she took her father's steel black clippers and raised them greatly, standing upright, statuesque, proud, finding strength on both sides of the mirror ... she looked lithic, as if she were about to salute, her father maybe, or maybe herself ...

She was feminine, and she was fortified ...

She killed herself that day, she killed the image of a child that had already been taken away, she killed the memory of a little girl that had been violated in the usual ways... she killed the woman everyone thought she'd grow to be ... she will no longer be afraid, she won't let them see only what they want to see ...

She took it to her head, ignited it and then, she started stripping away the layers of the world's expectancy of her sexual identity ... she shed away the dreaded jungle so that the world could see her crown ... and as her hair fell, though it could not be heard, there was a sound, there were legions rising, sirens crying, alarms were sounding, a one woman army would soon be marching ...

She saluted herself that day, she saluted herself in the mirror, and that's something that her father can never take away ...

Bitch this is your world, you found your own fucking way ...

Because, girls like this don't need heros, they need comrades in arms ...

She'll break the hold of gender roles,

She won't pay the toll, of beauty for gold

So say goodnight to the picturesque little good girl who killed herself that day ...

And say hello to this proud new symbol of woman, who found her own fucking way ...

D. Tori Morgenstein

Poetry Slam

All right, look, I need everyone to listen, cause I got something festering inside, that I must abide, and I can not conceal ... I'm gonna say something that may be harsh, may be crude but it's fucking real ... I ain't some pinata for you to take swings at after you get spun around like a wheel ... while you complain about the problems you couldn't solve, going on about how bad you feel ... you act like I owe you something more than understanding, but that's not the deal ... see at first all I wanted to do was earn the respect of your peers ... now all I want to do is rip your stupid poems up and scream in your ears ... people gasping, reacting like I brandished a weapon, but that's their own insecurity and fear ... acting like since I'm a hetero, anglo saxon male I'm an oppressor ... what the fuck, are you for real ...

Listen to this, women are not the only ones to be hurt by a man, we all have, just some of us can't show it or we're considered weak or not a man ... see, one night, at my old house, my old man, he tried to take my own life with his bare fucking hands, almost caved my chest in, I couldn't breath, I was sucking in air as hard as I can, all crying and shit staring up at the fan, trying to figure out what I did wrong, Dad, I'm sorry, damn ... but that was just another day in a life with my family man ...

I look at you people all dressed in black, wearing your pain as a dress, talking about the justice you lack.. Judging me for the words I use, rather than the content I pack ... me apologize, I don't have the fucking knack ... impropriety is just a part of me, I trade tack for obscurity, class for ingenuity, I may be miscreant but I stay true to me ... no apologies and nothing sacred, that's just me, color me jaded ... see, I don't owe you shit, you feeble freaks need to make up your fucking minds, stand up for something real, quit turning on a dime ... birds of a feather, yeah right, whatever ... in the end none of this shit really matters so step out of your fetters ... because in the end, we're all victims of incest and mental abuse, so you pointing your fingers at me, I have to ask, what the fuck is the use ...?

D. Tori Morgenstein

Judgment

I stand before you tonight
..........to be judged
...........judiciously judged
by Those that see THEMSELVES
.........fit
............to judge
Those that will judge Me
...by those unjust judgments
....past down upon Them......by Those
that saw THEMSELVES
....fit to judge
My LIFE
...has been one Judgment after another
by those that saw Themselves
...fit
.....to judge
I am judged by Judgment
.....Herself
.........Every day
judged by.... my hair
....By my clothes
..............my voice
judged by my sex
.....my steel
my skin
judged by My judgment
...or Lack there of
EVERYONE sees fit
...to judge Something
.......about Someone
.........Everyday
Those unjust judgments
Don't reflect upon Me
that which I judge

Myself
BUT RATHER
…. Reflect those Judgments
……….MY judges
have laid
….upon
THEMSELVES

Anthony F. Pepe

potential patricide

what the fuck
why would you
how could you
put him through all the shit you went through
are you jealous of his innocense?
Do you hate his smile?
Were you planing this sadistic bullshit all the while …?
His will you broke
His spirit you defile
what the fuck is with a man's hate for a child …

D. Tori Morgenstein

Dying Light

Sewer rat leech, reaches new
  heights, of levels of lows
  delved deeper than
While the Reaper is seen
  sewing cleaved hearts
  in rows, on cloak sleeves
Children lay weeping
  for words heard
  on bloody knees
Matron majestic
  mulling over manifestations
  that future brings
Futile fervor sings
  of festering angst
  with no defense against
Deceit received daily
  leaves faith, in hope
  denied as delusion
Involuntary invasions
  preemptive strike forces
  illicit no emotion
Slippery serpents
  no repent for
  solicitive salutations
Adoration admonished
  by *Amor*'s more
  counterproductive counterpart
Seemingly stoic
  though below
  teeming with accumulated turmoil

These things and more
  may bring

"the dying of the light," itself
to go willingly
"into that good night"

Anthony F. Pepe

Sunlight

The stormy skies of nature's bedroom eyes
    entice me, have past hence thrice vexed me
A moth to the flame it seems me insane
drawn to the eye of the storm
    in search of someplace warm
The lightning no longer frightens me
am hoping it will right me
The lashing sting of
    windswept rain on my face
All the pain needed
to keep me in my place
Songs sung by swollen seas
have me on my knees
A slave to the glory of its ways of fury
Dark clouds,
Death Shroud,
    shade eyes from true light
Bleary cold blustering winds from within
hold might over fright
Frozen crust on a pond holds me fond of
skating on thin ice
But storms still entice
To not see the beauty of the sunlight
Though I hear it looks rather nice

Anthony F. Pepe

69

This Is My Life

all these bubbles of air
kept frozen in their cells
freed by the poison in my drink
held prisoner by the ice
this is my life

beneath a weeping willow
lies a weeping warrior
freed by the poison in his drink
held prisoner by the strife
this is my life

how many moments will pass
until I realize this doesn't have to last
freed by the poison in my drink
held prisoner I think
this is my life

D. Tori Morgenstein

Bound

In the addict's attic
there hangs a long rope
tied with knots near
the end
Within these four walls
there's no need to pretend
that the corners are not dark
and no webs will suspend
What will, will be needed
to bring the nots
to the end
For, within this lone box
one, with no real locks
there is but one escape
one's own keys for to make
To unlock the nots
near the end
of a long rope
that hangs
In the addict's attic

Anthony F. Pepe

Remember Me This

Sleepless nights spent pondering
the plight of those wandering
predetermined courses
arriving with remorses

Wakeless sleep a dreaming
looking for some meaning
some worth I try to find
in what I'll leave behind

This mission may fruition be
solely me may only see
alone left standing
creating more misunderstanding

For in the end, the end
let it be said that I
most passionately did try

Anthony F .Pepe

Still Here

I am one thousand and three things
seen by two eyes
That could have sent three thousand and
One eyes blind
I am the wrist left unslit
and all the pain that it took, not to
I am watching the train, seventy mph
and all the strength needed, not to stop it
The dark hard line at the edge of the roof
and all the resolve it took not to cross it
The barrel of a gun left un-singed
by muzzle flash
and the last vestiges of virtue
that kept it so
The lost will
that will drive
on and on to the
last will
of a life left timely and full
I am dreams that dove down to
the depths of despair
to drag the flaming dragon
back to the surface for a breath of fresh air
I am the full bottle of pills on the shelf
and the shaky hand that left them there
I am
I am
I am
Still here

Anthony F. Pepe

Surrender

I probably, shoulda gave up, today
probably shoulda walked away today
I coulda, quit the fight, today
I woulda, shut my eyes, today
Coulda, shoulda, woulda
But I didn't, so I won't
Coulda, shoulda, woulda,
But I didn't, so I won't
I woulda shut my eyes today
Not to face the mirror and see
A man who had nothing to say
About the state of things to be
If we all, quit the fight, today
Coulda, shoulda, woulda,
But I didn't, so I won't
Coulda, shoulda, woulda,
But I didn't, so I won't
I'll not give up
I'll not forget
One's........
that did not get
to live to see......
Yesterday
They drive my hand
I take this stand
To change the lives
Around this man
I could have left this pain behind
looked around and tried to find
a way to leave the lost behind
Coulda, shoulda, woulda,
But I didn't, so I won't

Printed in the United States
34199LVS00004BA/240

9 781413 742183